Mari

THE POST COVID CHURCH

Thank you so much for your friendship & support over all these years! In Christ!

Stuart

"*The Post Covid Church* is a must read for all levels of today's church leaders. Stuart Kellogg has probed the best minds in practical ministry to produce a frank and honest look at the long-term effect of COVID on Christ's Body and, most importantly, the path forward. This powerful book will leave you surprised, challenged and inspired. It is a unique gift to the mission of Christ's Church."

—Hank Price | Author and Leadership Coach

"Stuart Kellogg takes the COVID pandemic seriously. But he takes more seriously God's work of caring for His Church and advancing His Kingdom. *The Post Covid Church* is not simply an emergency management program; it offers clear guidance in and through troubled times, to help church leaders and members keep focused on the hope of the Gospel and the promises of God. Stuart's vision is for the continuing work of seeking and advancing the Kingdom of God, of which the COVID pandemic is a temporary obstacle that believers can overcome by faith and obedience. Here you'll find sound advice for overcoming in the present together with renewed hope for overcoming until the Lord returns."

—T.M. Moore | Principal, The Fellowship of Ailbe

"The Pandemic didn't cause the malaise of the twentieth and twenty-first century church. It simply exposed the rot that was already there. We need answers that will bring us to a different posture and behavior. *The Post Covid Church* delivers answers!"

—Bishop Ronnie Crudup | Fellowship of International Churches

"The organized church was already declining, and now COVID-19 has accelerated its struggle. Stu does a great job of pointing out what got us to where we are, but also offers some great thoughts on how the Christian church can change so that it will not only survive but thrive. He encourages us to think about the awesome opportunity we have before us to live and share the good news to a world that desperately needs hope. As a retired pastor I recommend this book as a great read for any church leader."

—Phil Walker | President, Advance International

"Through the centuries external challenges facing the church have had a tremendous impact on the church's place and voice in society. COVID is arguably one of the top challenges facing the church in the past half-century. There are lots of unknowns and unanswered questions heading into the immediate future. Thankfully, Kellogg has attacked the issues surrounding the topic head on in *The Post Covid Church*. There's no doubt that this book will be a helpful resource for ecclesial leaders facing a broad range of new challenges brought on by the pandemic."

—Dr. Matt Ayars | President, Wesley Biblical Seminary

"In our current time of dealing with the COVID craziness, far too many pastors have been longing for a return to 'normal,' but I think they have forgotten too quickly that people were steadily leaving our churches during the 'normal' times. Fortunately, there are timeless biblical principles for giving us hope and direction during times like these.

Stuart Kellogg has studiously explored both the 'normal' practices of the pre-COVID church and the innovations of the mid-COVID church to bring us timeless applications that will serve the post-COVID church and its leaders well. Our ministries will never become effective if our ministry leaders are still clinging to ineffective 'normal' habits. This book will help us shake off the 'normal' practices and return to the timeless principles."

—Craig T. Owens | *Shepherd Leadership: The Metrics That Really Matter*

"In the midst of crisis, lies opportunity. That's the vision Stuart Kellogg saw as the pandemic began and the whole world changed. We can pretend the world will go back to the time prior to COVID-19, but that is not where the church needs to be. As faithful believers of the faith that was once delivered to the saints, we want to move into the next chapter with a game plan. Stuart helps us to begin thinking in that forward direction."

—Dr. Elaine Friedrich | Director, Digital Discipleship

THE POST COVID CHURCH

An Action Plan to THRIVE, Not Just Survive

Stuart Kellogg

ISBN 978-1-7355545-5-6

Library of Congress Control Number: 202191773

Printed in the United States of America

THE POST COVID CHURCH logo
designed by Andrew Silbert

Cover illustration: iStockphoto.com/Dimitris66
Author photo by Beth Kellogg

THE POST COVID CHURCH

thepostcovidchurch.com

For Beth, the love of my life.
For more than four decades, the rock
and inspiration who is the perfect
illustration of God's hand in my life.

ACKNOWLEDGEMENTS

First, above all, I want to thank my wife Beth who inspired me to use all the material from THE POST COVID CHURCH project and write this book. Without her support, editing and marketing help, this book would not be possible.

Joe Stradinger, you inspired me to take a few pages of commentary about how the church could more effectively react to the pandemic and turn it into THE POST COVID CHURCH social media project.

I had the honor of studying under Chuck Colson in what is now called the Colson Fellows Program as part of the Colson Center for Christian Worldview. T.M. Moore was the dean of the program when I attended and inspired me to dig deeper and to never strop striving to grow in my faith. T.M. is now Principal of The Fellowship of Ailbe and he has provided guidance, encouragement and prayer for this project since it began.

Dr. Phil Walker, a former pastor of mine, is such an inspiration and he has helped me focus my work so that it will have the most impact. So has Hank Price, who served as my mentor when we each ran TV stations for the Hearst Corporation. His strong faith guides all he does and his encouragement and support on this project are so appreciated. Bob Chandler, you put on that old consulting hat to help me think more strategically. Paul Ervin, your on-target critiques and encouragement helped keep me focused. S. Michael Craven, Dr. Todd Johnson and Eric Eilertsen, thank you for providing such helpful guidance in structuring the book's content.

To the men and women who took their time and allowed me to interview them for THE POST COVID CHURCH podcast, and whose inspiration and ideas are what this book is all about, it could not have been done without you.

A big thanks to Joe Lee and Cyndi Clark at Dogwood Press for all your help putting my words into published form.

Without the guidance from my Lord and Savior Jesus Christ, this project would never have begun. I pray there is an item or two that will help your church thrive and not just survive!

CONTENTS

INTRODUCTION 15

CHAPTER ONE
Accelerated Change 17

CHAPTER TWO
Turtle Churches 31

CHAPTER THREE
Leadership: "Run Towards the Roar" 49

CHAPTER FOUR:
Know What You Believe: Christian Worldview and Apologetics 69

CHAPTER FIVE
Image Problem: Time To Admit It and Take (often unpleasant) Stands 79

CHAPTER SIX
Not Just Surviving but THRIVING! 93

CONCLUSION 99

INDEX 107

INTRODUCTION

I've never worked on a church staff. I am, however, an evangelical Christian who has been an active lay leader, graduated from seminary and spent most of my career leading for-profit organizations. My greatest thrill is helping men and women succeed. I have spent more than a year interviewing dozens of church leaders from across the country, curating hundreds of stories and delving into key research projects so that I can present a collection of insights and best practices that will help THE POST COVID CHURCH come out of this pandemic thriving, not just surviving. I'm telling this story by using all the opportunities and insights I have learned from these men and women and sharing actionable steps to help your church fulfill its mission.

The American church faces unprecedented challenges in the wake of the pandemic and its resurgence. Members are leaving in droves, one-fourth of Americans do not identify as religious and the secular culture is intent on destroying the church's ability to have a voice in the public square.

We are spoiled in America. Too few of us realize that when Jesus promised that all believers will suffer for the faith, He meant us too! The world is watching. Despite the vitriol and saber-rattling of the secularists, deep down they are as afraid as anyone. Deep down they want to know if there is hope. Deep down they are wondering, "What is going on?" What a time to rise up and show them in a winsome and loving way. What a time for THE POST COVID CHURCH to live as Christ demands!

Is this the perfect time for another revival in America? The First and Second Great Awakenings swept through our country in the mid-eighteenth and early-nineteenth centuries, respectively, sparking revivals that increased an awareness of the faith, emphasized the need for personal redemption and accelerated church growth. Other revivals followed through the twentieth century, inspiring many in the midst of this COVID-19 pandemic to pray for another one.

Of course, unless followers of Christ live a transformed life and are not simply happy to be saved, there will be no revival. This does not minimize the importance of an individual's critical decision to follow Christ. Rather, it's a reminder that the body of Believers can't stop there. We must focus on growing in faith, dying to sin daily and taking up the cross of Christ. This way of life will show the world, and each other, that the living and powerful grace given to us means transformed lives as His hands and feet.

I pray that the ideas on these following pages will help your church become more salt and light for Christ in your community.

What a great time to lead a church!

CHAPTER ONE

Accelerated Change

The American church was already sick long before COVID-19 came ashore and turned our world upside down. The pandemic may have accelerated the change, but make no mistake, the American church, yes even the conservative evangelical church, was already hemorrhaging members and quickly losing influence in the culture. What THE POST COVID CHURCH faces now is an unprecedented challenge to return to its roots with leaders—lay and staff— focused on making disciples and honestly facing strong internal and external threats. What THE POST COVID CHURCH also has is an amazing opportunity to provide hope to a divided, angry and lost culture that will soon discover that it needs what we have to offer.

> **"There's never been a better time to be a church."**
>
> —Dr. Bill Wilson | Center for Healthy Churches

America came roaring out of its World War II victory over Nazi Germany and Japan. The Great Depression was just a memory as the economy exploded and the Baby Boom began. Unprecedented wealth did feed the image of prosperity for all, but beneath the surface things were not as rosy as they seemed. That is especially true when it comes to the stereotype of America as a homogeneous, God-fearing nation. The fact is, the romanticized picture of 1950s America filled with Bible-believing Christians, who all regularly attended church, never existed.

On the surface, the numbers told a positive story. A much larger percentage of Americans identified as Christians, were members of churches, and attended more regularly in the 1950s than now. In fact, three out of four Americans were church members in the 1950s. Church membership today is at an all-time low, with less than half of U.S. citizens saying they are members of a local congregation.

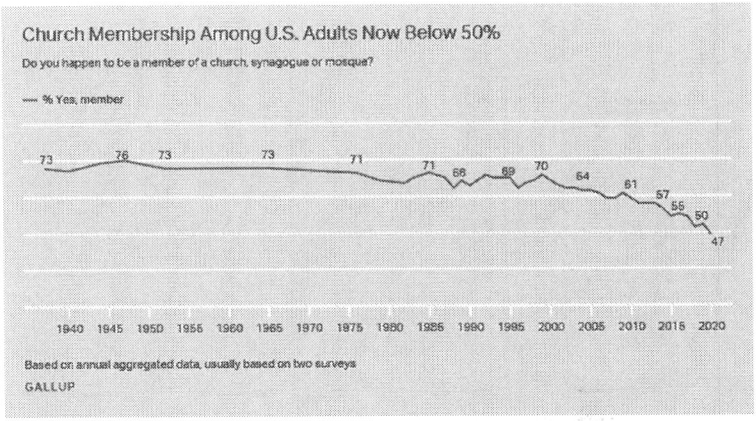

Gallup Polling [1]

It is also true that the church's *influence* in the American culture was far more powerful in generations past than it is now. Influence doesn't only mean the guardrails of common decency—think of laws restricting alcohol sales, the long process for divorce meant to encourage couples to stay together to benefit the children, and pornography relegated to the seedy parts of town—but also basic biblical knowledge. The average American was exposed to biblical truth *through* culture, not in spite of it. Since neighbors were more likely to attend church, there was a bigger chance of hearing the Gospel. Someone who had only been to church for weddings and funerals still heard the Gospel through Bible readings in his public school, or hearing Linus recite the story of Christ's birth from Luke's

1 Jeffrey M Jones, "U.S. Church Membership Falls Below Majority for First Time," news.gallup.com, Gallup, *https://news.gallup.com/poll/341963/church-membership-falls-below-majority-first-time.aspx*, 3.29.21

Gospel in the annual "A Charlie Brown Christmas" special on CBS. Foundational biblical basics were generally understood.

The church, Protestant and Roman Catholic alike, also held a respectable position in the culture. Whether one attended church or not, the minister and priest were held up as exemplars of decorum and clean living. The contrast between the opinion of clergy now compared to just forty years ago is an apt illustration. Those holding a "high/very high" opinion of the honesty and ethical standards of pastors has dropped from 67% to only 37% in the last forty years, the lowest mark since Gallup began asking the question in 1977.

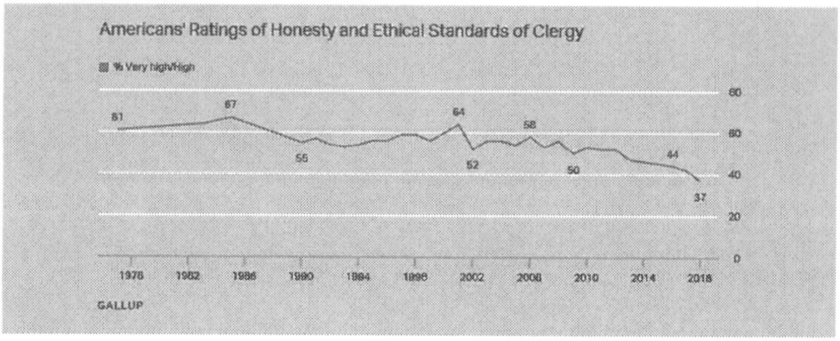

Gallup Survey [2]

The 1950s is memorialized in movies and TV commercials with the white married parents and children happily working, cleaning and playing. The decade was, in fact, the beginning of the church's slide. The post-war material

2 Megan Brenan, "Nurses Again Outpace Other Professions for Honesty, Ethics," news.gallup.com, Gallup, *https://news.gallup.com/poll/245597/nurses-again-outpace-professions-honesty-ethics.aspx*, 12.20.2018

boom meant unprecedented home ownership, a rapidly expanding middle class and mass suburban migration. Manufacturing exploded as the rest of the industrial world recovered from the devastating war. While attending church was acceptable (and even expected as part of the post-war American portrait), little-noticed currents were rapidly churning and undermining biblical faith.

The mainline Protestant denominations were slowly but steadily moving away from traditional, orthodox belief. The mainline seminaries were rejecting Christ's exclusive truth claims—and in some cases His deity. What were once understood and accepted basic biblical principals were now looked down upon as the simpleton beliefs of the fundamentalists and the ignorant. What took its place?

In his book *How Should We Then Live*, theologian Francis Schaeffer writes that as the post-war, consumer-driven culture saw the Christian-dominated consensus weaken, the nation adopted personal peace and affluence as the primary values. The impact on the children was powerful, as we saw when the boomers came of age in the 1960s. "The young people want more to life than *personal peace* and *affluence*. They were right in their analysis of the problem, but they were mistaken in their solutions," Schaeffer writes.[3]

Schaeffer notes that children rebelled to find more "meaning". Rather than embracing God or the concept of "absolute truth", they turned to drugs and an assault

3 Francis A. Schaeffer, *How Should We Then Live*, (Wheaton, Ill., Crossway Books, 2005), pp 208

on "authority". Pastor and writer Mark Sayers writes in *Disappearing Church* that the counterculture "rebellion against all inherited authority led to the enshrinement of the individual as the highest authority....The counter-cultural revolution had morphed into a therapeutic quest to discover individual fulfillment."[4]

By the 1970s, "taking drugs was no longer an ideology," Shaeffer wrote.[5] It was simply an escape. The pill suddenly made sex a lifestyle, while the no-fault divorce law signed by California Governor Ronald Reagan was rapidly replicated across the nation and greased the skids for the dissolution of the traditional family.

The mainline denominations started their steady decline as a result of embracing the social Gospel and rejecting many foundational tenets of the Christian faith, while the evangelical church exploded in the seventies. Presidential candidate Jimmy Carter famously spoke openly about his "born again" faith. Suddenly, many of those living outside the "Bible Belt" were introduced through the secular media to this proposition. Growing up as a mainline Presbyterian, I'd never heard a minister talk about having a personal relationship with Christ. In the wake of the political upheaval surrounding the Watergate break-in and resignation of President Richard Nixon, a serious politician like Carter explaining that he was a sinner, saved by grace and promising to bring integrity to the White House, was

---

4 Mark Sayers, *Disappearing Church: From Cultural Relevance to Gospel Resilience*, (Chicago, Moody Publishers, 2016), pp 32

5 Schaeffer, *How Should*, pp 205

powerful.

The fact that President Carter's policies alienated so many conservatives led to Rev. Jerry Falwell's "Moral Majority" in the mid-1970s, creating an unholy marriage between the Republican Party and evangelicals. This more aggressive political stance by conservatives coincided with Republicans rapidly expanding their power into the South. The Democratic party became more liberal, more ethnically diverse and more centered in large cities and the coasts. By the time President George W. Bush was running for his second term in 2004, his political machine effectively made conservative Christians a wing of the Republican party and alienated half the electorate.

The political divide accelerated through President Barack Obama's eight years in office. Actions such as implementing the Affordable Care Act (also known as "Obama Care") ignited the Tea Party movement of conservatives that pushed the Republican Party even more to the right. By the time COVID-19 arrived, the identification between white evangelicals and Republicans was overwhelming: white evangelicals make up about one out of four Americans, but almost four out of five voted for President Trump in 2020.[6] Once the evangelical church lost its willingness and ability to speak "truth to power", and instead fell in line like any other political constituency, the ability to appeal to the lost was profoundly diminished.

The reality is, rather than simply speaking to those who

6 Elana Schor and David Crary, "AP VoteCast: Trump wins White Evangelicals, Catholics Split", AP Votecast, *https://apnews.com/article/votecast-trump-wins-white-evangelicals-d0cb249ea7eae29187a21a702dc84706*, 11.06.2020

haven't heard the Good News, the church is now facing a growing, much more antagonistic group of Americans with little or no biblical understanding and a desire to strangle Christianity's influence in the nation. We see that in the state prosecution against Colorado Christian Jack Phillips, who was sued because he refused to use his talents to create a cake for a same-sex couple. He never refused to serve anyone his baked goods; he simply refused to create a special cake. While he won on a narrow technicality, he and others who refuse to buckle under continue to be sued and harassed. This is not surprising, because now more than one out of five Americans have no religious connection, and more than half of Americans don't belong to a church.[7]

The problem is more acute among the young. They are not only less likely to attend church, the vast majority of millennials (those between 24-40) don't partake in the basics of Christian disciplines such as prayer or studying the Bible.[8] Even among practicing *Christian millennials,* almost half believe evangelism is wrong![9]

This is the time for Believers to look in the mirror, quit condemning those outside the faith and ask, "How can we live out this life-changing faith in Christ in a way that attracts and does not repel?"

---

7 Jones, "U.S. Church Membership"

8 Pew Research Center, *https://www.pewforum.org/religious-landscape-study/generational-cohort/younger-millennial/*, 3.21.2019

9 Barna Research, "Almost Half of Practicing Christian Millennials Believe Evangelism is Wrong," *https://www.barna.com/research/millennials-oppose-evangelism/*, 2.05.2019

Of course, "the church" is not a monolith. The Southern Baptist and Episcopalian churches across the street from each other disagree on the most fundamental aspects of the faith. The reason both are losing members and influence in the culture, however, must be faced, or THE POST COVID CHURCH will become as influential as the Elks Club.

"Jesus' views are offensive; we shouldn't be."

The Barna research group reported in 2020 that one-third of church-goers stopped attending in person, or even online, after the nationwide shutdown.[10] In fact, one analysis concluded that for the last decade, between 3,850 and 7,700 churches closed each year, and estimated the rate would *triple* in the next few years.[11] It's not just the more liberal mainline denominations losing members; in fact, the Southern Baptist Convention, the largest Protestant denomination in America with fourteen million members, has lost more than two million since 2006.[12] Once out of the habit, millions of mainliners and evangelicals have decided it wasn't worth it to return.

It's also clear that holding basic biblical beliefs is more costly than ever in America, with government and private

10 Barna: State of the Church, "One in Three Practicing Christians Has Stopped Attending Church During COVID", *https://www.barna.com/research/new-sunday-morning-part-2/*, 7.08.2020

11 Richard Reinhard, International City/Count Management Association, "Redeveloping Houses of Worship," 04.01.2021

12 Bob Smietana, "Southern Baptist Decline Continues," Religion News Service, *https://religionnews.com/2021/05/21/southern-baptist-decline-continues-denomination-has-lost-more-than-2-million-members-since-2006/*, 5.21.2021

companies being increasingly forceful in their opposition. There is no better example than the issue of transgender rights. States passing laws that, for example, say children born male can't compete in female athletics are facing major attacks. In fact, seventy major companies have signed a statement condemning what they call anti-LGBTQ legislation, and the state of California banned state-funded travel to any state that has passed similar laws.[13] No debate—just charges of hate.

Even the foundational protections found in our First Amendment are under attack. The proposed "Equality Act", passed by the U.S. House in early 2021, strips protections for religious organizations, thereby severely limiting religious freedoms found in the Bill of Rights. While unlikely to pass the U.S. Senate in the foreseeable future, the fact that a majority of House members would so cavalierly toss aside such a bedrock of the Republic is breathtaking.[14] This as the Little Sisters of the Poor continue to fight against the federal government forcing them to pay for contraception and abortifacients.

So, yes, in the wake of the pandemic, the American culture is far more hostile to churches and Believers that hold

---

13 "Major U.S. Companies Continue to Oppose Anti-Transgender State Legislation, *Freedom For All Americans, https://freedomforallamericans.org/over-55-major-u-s-companies-oppose-anti-transgender-state-legislation/*, 04.20.2021; "California Bans Travels to Florida and 4 Other States", Associated Press/NPR, *https://www.npr.org/2021/06/29/1011253354/california-bans-state-travel-to-florida-and-4-other-states-lgbtq*, 6.29.2021

14 Ed Stetzer, "The Equality Act Is the Most Significant Threat to Religious Liberty in a Generation," Church Leaders, *https://churchleaders.com/news/391080-the-equality-act-is-the-most-significant-threat-to-religious-liberty-in-a-generation.html*, 02.26.2021

foundational Biblical beliefs. The mainline churches that have embraced the "spirit of the age" in an effort to be "relevant" may have escaped the hostility, but find their membership decimated. They also find themselves alienating many of those who *reject* the Christian faith! Writer Jonathon Van Maren says that even some of the most strident *non-believers* are admitting that there is tremendous value to the culture from Christianity.

"Douglas Murray, the conservative writer who was raised in the Church before leaving it as an adult, has occasionally referred to himself as a 'Christian atheist.' In a recent discussion with theologian N.T. Wright, he described himself as 'an uncomfortable agnostic who recognizes the virtues and the values the Christian faith has brought,' and noted that he is actually irritated by the way the Church of England is fleeing from its inheritance, 'giving up its jewels' such as 'the King James Bible and The Book of Common Prayer' in exchange for progressive pieties.

"My fear is that the Church is not doing what so many of us on the outside want it to do, which is preaching its gospel, asserting its truths and its claims," he (Murray) said. "When one sees it falling into all the latest tropes, one thinks, 'Well, that's another thing gone, just like absolutely everything else in the era.' I'm a disappointed non-adherent."[15]

What these thinking atheists, including Scottish historian Niall Ferguson, realize is that even if they don't believe, they are a lot better off—and safer—-by living in a

---

15 Jonathon Van Maren, "The Turning Tide of Intellectual Atheism," MercatorNet, *https://mercatornet.com/the-turning-tide-of-intellectual-atheism/72999/*, 06.29.2021

culture that follows Christ.

"I know I can't achieve religious faith," Ferguson told Van Maren, "but I do think we should go to church. We don't have, I don't think, an evolved ethical system. I don't buy the idea that evolution alone gets us to be moral. It can modify behavior, but there's just too much evidence that in the raw, when the constraints of civilization fall away, we behave in the most savage way to one another. I'm a big believer that with the inherited wisdom of a two-millennia-old religion, we've got a pretty good framework to work with."[16]

The most honest of the atheists also know that it is those who act as the hands and feet of Christ who stand out. After Hurricane Katrina ravaged the Mississippi Gulf Coast in 2005 and subsequently caused the massive levee breaks in New Orleans, British writer and atheist Roy Hattersley was wonderfully honest as he saw the army of Christian servants rushing to help those in need: "Notable by their absence are teams from rationalist societies, free thinkers' clubs and atheists' associations—the sort of people who not only scoff at religion's intellectual absurdity but also regard it as a positive force for evil."[17]

The good news: like ripping the Band-Aid off, the pandemic simply forces the church to get much of the pain out of the way quickly. To face the reality that for much of the U.S., the biblical message is *missing the mark*. Those

---

16 Ibid

17 Roy Hattersley, "Faith Does Breed Charity", The Guardian, *https://www.theguardian.com/world/2005/sep/12/religion.uk*, 09.11.2005

who really weren't devoted to what the church stands for have wandered off. The reality that many church leaders were not facing is now quite stark. As you will read, the pandemic gives us a glimpse of how churches must act if they are to thrive. It also shows us that weak leaders and a timid outlook are going to make far too many congregations irrelevant ... then invisible.

What an exciting time to be a church, indeed. So many needs ... so many ideas to serve those needs ... so many opportunities to show the world that followers of Christ are committed to giving, just as Christ has given.

CHAPTER TWO

Turtle Churches

The pandemic simply accelerated the already palpable decline of the American church. It is not just numbers—it is members, churches, attendance. The church's influence has steadily waned in the face of increased hostility. The silver lining from the pandemic is that it forces churches to quickly pivot. To not change is not an option if the church is to fulfill its mission—to make disciples.

> **"Whether it will lead to a revival, it certainly focused the mind."**
>
> —T.M. Moore | The Fellowship of Ailbe

THE POST COVID CHURCH project began because I saw a sharp demarcation between those "turtle churches" that hunkered down, pulled in and waited for "normal" to return, and those that saw this as an *opportunity* to be the hands and feet of Christ. There really weren't any churches in the middle. I was frustrated seeing those church leaders who refused to grasp the opportunity, and so impressed with leaders from tiny and large churches who were *acting.* What began as an essay grew into a multi-pronged social media campaign, thanks to entrepreneur Joe Stradinger. The mission is simple: *Helping the church share more of the Good News in the face of persecution, hostility and disinterest.* How can churches possibly do that if they aren't reaching out?

The downsides of social media are well known. The upside is that with the internet, cheap cameras and only elementary knowledge, churches quickly moved online when the doors were shut. In fact, it's estimated that between 80-90% of churches, large and small, streamed at least one service a week. The turtle churches stopped there; the churches positioned to thrive used old and new technology to hyper-connect with their members and reach out beyond their walls.

Pinelake is a megachurch in Mississippi, with six campuses across the state. The technical sophistication, honed by years of streaming the pastor's message from the home base in Brandon, meant it was easier to pivot technologically during the crisis. While the worship service is entirely pre-produced, viewers can interact live, one-on-one, with staff and trained laity. This means answering prayer requests—and just talking. This is cutting edge, but not the focus for senior pastor Chip Henderson. "When you're socially distant and can't gather, the entire staff turned to caring for and ministering to the entire family. We started calling elderly adults and single moms, then spread out and called every member." That's ten thousand members, called more than once. "There were wonderful God moments. People said, 'I can't believe you called me today, of all days.'"

The use of the telephone to simply connect with those at home, especially the elderly, was such a simple method. Yet I can't tell you how many shared with me the frustration of not hearing from anyone at their churches, not even once. As one member told me, "The staff is getting paid their salaries, no one is coming to church. What are they doing all day?"

Tools allowing us to worship from the comfort of our home have also been used by innovative leaders to reach out, even in the poorest places in the world. Haitian pastor Dr. Lucner Pierre chose to expand Bible studies through the internet, and rather than 50-100 turning up, more than 1,000 connected. Many were not just listening to the study, but asking questions. "We touched more people, not just in Haiti," Dr. Pierre told me. "Because of poverty problems, we have many Haitians who leave the country to live in other places in the world and we lost connection with those people. But since we've transferred online, we got connected with those people again." The great commission in action: making disciples through technology and touching those hungry for the Word.

ACTION ITEM

As we've seen during the Delta resurgence, COVID will be with us for a long time. That could very well mean more shutdowns. Has your church set up a system to connect with all the members next time the doors shut? Even when you reopen, what happens when a church member doesn't show up in the service or small group for two weeks? This should be a focus point. The body of Christ is to support and care. Setting up a system to track members is simpler than ever. There must be a commitment from the top to do so and there must be follow-up. How powerful would it be to hear from the pastor? There are also plenty of members willing to reach out. In this social media society, real relationships are harder than ever to cultivate and grow. Using the "old school" method of a quick call will do wonders.

> **“We now live in a Post-Christian culture.”**
>
> —Dr. Elaine Friedrich | Director, Digital Discipleship

In a suburb of Atlanta, Georgia, Dr. Elaine Friedrich is an example of a strong leader who is thinking forward, counting on more disruption and planning for a very different future. Dr. Friedrich's career blends ministry and higher education leadership into her current position as Director of Digital Discipleship for Mt. Bethel United Methodist Church in Marietta, Georgia. While her church is large, with more than 9,000 members, she's helped churches of all sizes see that they need to shift focus and resources if they want to stay connected with their members and fulfill the great commission. It's what Dr. Friedrich calls seeing "what is possible".

"If you're at a congregation that may not have had any kind of digital platform prior to this, you may think this is not a one-time thing," she told me. "This is something that will be going on. We now live in a post-Christian culture. We're actually living in exile right now, so how can we reach members of our congregation and beyond so others might know the Gospel; reach the least, the last and the lost? To be able to do that, you may need to shift resources around to where that does become an important part of the church's missional opportunity. So that as we develop and think through what our next five or ten years look like, that we're very intentional about including not just face-to-face, the way we've always done it, but we're including ways to connect people digitally. Do it in ways that will engage people and build relationships whether you're in the same room or around the world somewhere. So that's the joy of it."

ACTION ITEM

Has your church done more than simply stream services? While not replacing the personal touch, creative use of technological media can supplement in-person contact and provide a bridge to stay connected even when traveling. It's also a way to more effectively stay engaged with younger members of your church.

No matter how effective the technology, there is no replacing one-on-one connections. The first churches are a testament to the power of Believers gathering together. The psychological toll from pandemic-induced isolation is devastating. The Kaiser Family Foundation reports that during the pandemic, about four out of ten adults in the U.S. reported symptoms of anxiety or depressive disorder. That's *four times* the number just a year before the pandemic-mandated shutdowns. One out of three said they had difficulty sleeping and eating, with one out of eight admitting they were consuming more alcohol and illicit drugs.[18]

> **"Isolation is a diabolical form of torture."**
> —Dr. David Wadner I Psychologist

Helping neighbors—in the church and outside—must be a focus of THE POST COVID CHURCH. The needs are widening, the results destructive and widespread. Community is at the heart of a church body and is perfectly positioned to help. Psychologist Dr. Tarama Fleming is a licensed professional counselor in private practice who strongly believes the Christian faith is uniquely positioned to heal, and she and challenges THE POST COVID CHURCH to support those in emotional need.

"A lot of people are telling me in counseling sessions that they're feeling lonely; it's causing them a lot of mental distress such as depressed moods. They have a lot of fear and anxiety because of the uncertainly about how this is going to turn out, about the future and the unknown. They also report a lot of resentment and bitterness during this time. A lot of people have friends and family that they're no longer speaking to because of politics. Now more than

18 Nirmita Panchal, et.al., "The Implications of COVID-19 For Mental Health and Substance Use," Kaiser Family Foundation, *https://www.kff.org/coronavirus-covid-19/issue-brief/the-implications-of-covid-19-for-mental-health-and-substance-use/*, 02.10.2021

ever the body of Christ needs the support of the church, the presence of the church to continue. We need more now; we need the church to intervene in this crisis. We need a continued presence for small groups, door-to-door ministry, phone ministry; whatever they can do to reach out to people and find out what their needs are."

Dr. Fleming is passionate about the need to respond because she sees the impact of isolation and fear up close. She also is well aware that far too many in the church are wary of even speaking about mental health, especially, she says, in the African American church.

"There's such a stigma attached to mental health that when people are in crisis, they try to keep it within the family or handle it on their own. In my experience, a lot of African American churches do not seek out mental health counseling or encourage it. More often than not, we want to cast out demons; we don't encourage following up with professional counseling and I believe it's very important that we do that.

"As believers we should continue our spiritual disciplines: prayer, fasting, morning and evening routines such as devotional time, journal writing, being in gratitude or Biblical meditation. It's important to get involved in extra activities your church is offering. You want to keep moving and being around other people."

Rev. Percy McCray, Jr. spent two decades as a hospital chaplain counselor, and the last seven years as Director of Faith-Based Programs at Cancer Treatment Centers of America. He's certainly not alone in the profession when he says he's never seen a year like 2020. He is optimistic, however, because he knows the power of the Christian faith can help one overcome mental stress *if* THE POST COVID CHURCH changes how it approaches mental health.

"One of the areas the faith community has not done a very good job of is addressing the dynamic of mental health. I know with regards to the cultural orientation and background I come from (African American churches), very little was ever discussed about mental health from a faith-based perspective. It was always within the context of, 'Hey, use your faith. We're going to pray this away. Get in the Word. Make sure you have good gospel music going on to kind of help counteract that.' The reality is, if nothing else, COVID has forced us to invest in this idea of mental wellness and mental health being a reality for us."

The fact is, the simplest interaction can have more of an impact than a therapy session. "Isolation is a diabolical form of torture. The more isolated, the more trauma results," says Dr. David Wadner, a retired clinical psychologist who spent his entire career treating patients in the Chicago area. "Particularly dangerous for children and the elderly. Healthy, stable adults will begin to experience depression after a surprisingly short amount of isolation."

Rather than relying exclusively on professional help, Dr. Wadner says churches should think simpler. "I don't think professionals are necessarily always the first answer. What we all need is to return to the level of socialization that provided us with a sense of connectedness and belonging. I think the church reaching out to its members is the first step, even if it's just a phone call. Let them know they aren't forgotten, that they are still a valuable part of the collective. This will help reestablish a sense of psychological equilibrium."

ACTION ITEM

How often do churches focus on mental health? Like the rest of culture, too many churches see it as a subject best taken care of in the shadows. This is the perfect time to put mental health front and center. More suicides, depression and isolation cry out for solutions. What organization is better suited to provide support? Biblically-based programs and education for parents are widely available. This is not a "secular" concern, nor is treating mental illness anti-faith. The problem is getting worse. What a time for the church to stand out! How best can your church leverage those Christians in the mental health profession in your area? Are there professionals in your pews? Just speaking and preaching about the problem will make a big difference. So, too, will Christians simply calling and visiting those who are alone. Isolation will not change once the pandemic recedes.

> **"If you aren't going to serve, this church isn't for you."**
>
> —Pastor Robert Hahn | Chesapeake Church

Chesapeake Church in rural Maryland isn't for everyone. In fact, senior pastor Robert Hahn is very blunt about that. He believes by serving, scripture comes alive, and he knows that folks who simply come to sing, pray and leave will feel very uncomfortable very quickly. That's just fine with him.

"A lot of people get upset when I say that to them," Robert told me. "But we do say to them, 'Look, if your idea of church is to come sit here, sing a few songs and hear a message and go home, we're not the right church for you. You can attend, obviously, but after a few years, the pressure will bear down on you.'"

Chesapeake Church has always served the community, often in very creative ways. For example, it hosts regular "oil change" days for single moms. Why? One of the last things a harried mom caring for kids and working thinks about is the regular maintenance of a car. Yet if the car breaks down, her life is suddenly in crisis mode. It is an example of a simple way to connect and help. Hundreds in the church are regularly part of a wood giveaway because so many in this rural area still heat with wood-burning stoves. The church's "serving DNA" meant that when the COVID shutdown came, the church did not miss a beat.

In fact, it saw a huge opportunity because 1,300 needy children in the county were suddenly facing no breakfast or lunch. The school system set up grab-and-go locations, but with no public transportation, Robert knew the rural poor were going to go hungry.

"We mobilized immediately and started to purchase large quantities of what are called shelf-stable foods, and foods that didn't need to be refrigerated. Also, foods that young kids could microwave. We purchased large amounts of it, creating what we call 'kids kits', which provide essentially four meals which we can take them for two days. That's how we started."

"They're delivering food to the doors that they used to kick in."

How to get the food to the kids? An ingenious idea that solved two problems:

"We had the student resource officers who now had nothing to do because their schools were closed," Robert told me. "The sheriff gave them to us as a resource, and they began delivering the meals right to the doors of these young kids."

That's right, the police were now the solution to these poor people's problems.

"They're coming in their police cruisers. They used to get booed and now they get applauded, because they're delivering food to the doors that they used to kick in. It's been very transformative for the entire community and people have really noticed it. So now the Gospel is going out the way Jesus did it, by feeding people and caring for people."

The church was already providing food for the needy in southern Maryland, so to pivot quickly was a bit easier. It only happens, however, because of strong leadership and a vision to serve. It also happens alongside ministry partners. Yes, *collaboration* while living as the hands and feet of Christ. Chesapeake Church has 73 partners, with 43 of them part of the food distribution efforts.

ACTION ITEM

Pastor Robert Hahn says most of the ideas come from church members, not from staff. His leadership style invites the laity to not just serve, but provide ideas and leadership. Now, copying the church's firewood giveaway won't do a lot in South Florida, but are there needs your church can serve now for those falling through the cracks? Are there opportunities to collaborate with other organizations? Are there members of your church who are working with non-profits that could use the help?

Sometimes the solutions to a need come from the most unusual places and involve amazing ingenuity. Rev. Rusty Rabon leads the 180-member Grace Chapel in West Columbia, South Carolina. The church has a significant number of elderly people who Rusty knew could not safely return as the doors reopened. Many were also not able to stream. The solution?

Build a radio station.

"We were very fortunate to have an engineer with the South Carolina Educational Television System. He was able to secure for us a small analog transmitter. He and another engineer friend of his fabricated an antenna for us. The signal was going out about a mile from the church."

This meant members could listen on their FM radios if they lived nearby. Others not comfortable going inside drove into the church parking lot to listen. Not exactly the type of thing a lot of churches could do, but an amazing illustration of what happens when the focus is on fulfilling a need!

Dr. Phil Walker has a unique perspective. He retired after twenty-nine years as a Southern Baptist pastor but remains President of Advance International, an organization that for fourteen years has taught local Christians in China, Indonesia, Latin America and elsewhere to be pastors. He's been able to reflect on what churches are doing (and not doing) during the pandemic. One of the key recommendations he has is for church leadership to reassess *everything*, from the size of staff to job descriptions. Most important to Dr. Walker is focusing on the needs. Here are some of the recommendations from his list he called "What If I Was Still A Pastor":

ACTION ITEMS

- Find the community needs—financial, transportation, child care, food, training—and meet them.
- Get the word out through social media, public relations and advertising to let the community know the church is providing hope in the middle of tough times.
- Connect with mission partners; even find new ones. Focus on helping those who are in the "trenches" and helping the most needy.
- Tie outreach to a sermon series on Hope, so the church knows what's at stake and is encouraged to be part of the solution.
- Encourage members to be more intentional about finding people at their work, school, community and clubs who are in need. Connect them to the church's efforts to meet those needs.
- Make sure members are led to be disciple makers and not just disciples.

Dr. Matt Friedeman teaches at Wesley Biblical Seminary. He planted and pastors an evangelical church in Clinton, Mississippi, and spent years as a radio talk show host and newspaper columnist. He's written twelve books on discipleship and mission—and it is hard to put him in a nice, simple cultural box. Progressives hearing his conservative political views are floored when they find out that Matt has spent decades ministering in prisons, regularly inviting released inmates to the racially integrated church he leads. For Matt, the two go together biblically. He regularly encourages Christ followers to get involved but found out that the title of his former radio show, *In The Fight*, was sometimes misunderstood.

"I remember doing that radio program one day, and a guy called up and says, 'Hey, Matt, I'm in the fight with you, man!' I said, 'You are? I want to know what you are doing in the fight.' He said, 'Well, I'm listening to you.' So in his mind, listening to talk radio was being in the fight. Listening to talk radio is *not* being in the fight. Listening to your preacher is *not* being in the fight. Going to church is *not* being in the fight."

Matt always stresses that it is what we do with the Gospel after we *leave* church that matters.

"Martin Luther used a Latin phrase to define sin that is translated, 'A heart curved in on itself.' What's the opposite of that? A heart curved out to other people. A heart curved in is a definition of sin. The definition of righteousness is a heart curved out to human need."

Matt loves to use the image of water—living water—as an analogy to serving. He stresses that all followers of Christ are demanded to serve.

"When water comes from someplace, where does it go? It goes to the lowest place. In our culture, right now, we need that message more than ever. Living water, the Spirit within us, flowing to the darkest places of our culture.

"That is why I've tried to get as many people as possible from my church involved in sharing love at the abortion clinic. I'd like for them to go to the prisons, to go to the nursing homes, to set up Bible clubs in a public school. I mean, just let's get out there! Let's have our hearts curved out to other people where they can know the healing God wants us all to know. We are now the temples where living water come from and then flows into the places that desperately need healing. And boy, we need healing."

Captain Ken Chapman is the Orlando, Florida, Area Commander for the Salvation Army. Before the pandemic, Ken and his Army team regularly served hundreds of the elderly, disabled, homeless and at-risk youth each day. Shortly after the shutdown, he and his team quickly swung into motion, knowing that the tourist-dependent area would be hammered for months. A 5,200-square-foot tent with portable showers was erected to house the homeless while demand for basic services almost tripled. A silver lining to the pandemic is that Ken, a fourth generation Salvationist, believes there will be more church cooperation.

"The problem with the church and every appointment I've had with the Salvation Army: the churches and the communities love us. Many of them support our mission and the things we're doing and contribute to us. But churches tend to be very territorial, including the Salvation Army. Everyone has their own mission, everyone has their own focus. Sometimes it's difficult to get cooperation. Now, however, we're seeing that many of them are coming to help us. We're seeing much more openness of the denominations and churches coming together. We're having to share this together. We are realizing that together, we're stronger than when we do things individually."

It's sort of biblical!

The early church exploded because the people saw Christians giving themselves sacrificially. Chuck Colson provides a vivid example in his book *The Faith*. In second-century Roman cities, plagues were a common occurrence with squalid conditions and close living providing the perfect breeding grounds. When the plagues came, the wealthy left for the country and 30-40% of the city inhabitants died from disease. Imagine seeing groups of people not fleeing, but rushing *towards* those highly contagious with pus-covered smallpox sores! The ministry was dangerous, but as Colson wrote:

"The care Christians showed often did result in them succumbing to the plague themselves. But paradoxically, their compassion did not deplete Christian ranks in the long term—quite the reverse. Tending to the sick increased the disease survival rate by as much as two-thirds, and this witness attracted many new converts. By acting on the teachings of Christ, without regard to their own welfare, the Christians, against all expectations, progressed from being a small sect to a dominant cultural group."[19]

The world is watching. The world is in need. What a powerful difference the church makes when the members live out their faith as servants for Christ—together!

19 Charles Colson, *The Faith* (Grand Rapids, MI, Zondervan, 2008) pp 17

CHAPTER THREE

Leadership: "Run Towards the Roar"

The difference between a turtle church and one reaching out during the pandemic is simple to identify: Leadership. From the top.

The pandemic has quickly identified those equipped and willing to lean in and answer a crisis—and those too comfortable, who think they can simply wait out the storm and get back to normal. The reality: there's no "normal" in which to return. In any case, why on earth would the American church want to do that?

T.M. Moore is Principal of The Fellowship of Ailbe, a spiritual fellowship in the Celtic Christian tradition. He's written more than thirty books, including *Revive Me*. He succinctly explained during a podcast interview why "returning to normal" is a non-starter:

"We were losing ground. We were not making any impact to speak of on the culture or on the major issues of our society. We were just sort of content going about our business doing our little church thing and not bothering anybody. And so why would we ever want to go back there and just keep doing *that*?"

Now is the perfect time for assessment. The strongest organizations regularly review what they are doing, how they are doing it and how to improve. It should be clear by now that simply going through the motions will not work. It also means instead of cowering in the face of challenges, THE POST COVID CHURCH must engage—assertively. John Robertson is an ordained pastor with the Evangelical Christian Churches in Canada. After decades of experience leading churches, he transitioned to crisis management and also helps men and women discover God's PLAN© for their lives through his FORTLOG Services company.

"When the lion roars, the normal instinct is instead of running towards the roar, we run away from it or freeze. But quite often when we run away from the roar, we run into the hunting party. So when we give flight, we actually run right into the hunting party and then have bigger problems. If we are to choose to live by faith, by a relationship with Christ—not churchianity religion—that means that Christ is calling us to run towards the roar. What does it mean for God to be with me no matter what happens? What does it mean to run towards the roar? That requires a complete reframe of what does it mean to 'Fear not, for I am with you.' (Isaiah 41:10) Because if He is with me through anything, then what is it that He doesn't do?"

> **"Churches pick based on teaching and preaching, not leadership."**
>
> —Dr. George Barna

It takes real leadership to make this approach part of your church's DNA. Dr. George Barna, called the most quoted man in the church today, has spent more than a generation surveying Americans about their faith. He has also pastored churches and used the data he's acquired to help leaders more effectively fulfill the church's mission: to make disciples. He is now the Director of Research at Arizona Christian University's Cultural Research Center. He told me he's more concerned than ever about church leadership. One of the biggest obstacles: church staff refusing to identify and use the talent in the pews.

"Leaders must encourage talented people in the pews. What a great leader does is empower other people to identify God's vision and calling for their life. Then to give them the resources and the opportunities they need to pursue that vision that God has uniquely for that person. If we had a church in America where God's called leaders were allowed to empower people in that manner, and to get them motivated and enthusiastic about it, and to celebrate the victories that those people are having in their pursuit of God's calling and purpose for their lives, the church in America would be absolutely unstoppable. It would be the thing that everybody would want to be part of."

Dr. Barna says when hiring senior pastors, too much emphasis is placed on teaching and preaching. The result is weak leaders who are not focusing on the right things. For example, he says the typical senior pastor judges whether their church is effective by measuring attendance, giving, the size of the staff, number of programs and the amount of built-out square footage. That, he says, is a problem.

"Jesus didn't die for any of those things. He didn't die to put butts in seats. He didn't die to give the church the biggest real estate portfolio in the community. He died to see lives transformed. So our measures of effectiveness and ministry really need to go back to transformation. Jesus told His disciples, 'They'll know you're my disciples when you obey my teaching, when you love one another and when you produce spiritual fruit.' Those are the things we need to be measuring."

To truly transform itself, Dr. Barna says THE POST COVID CHURCH has to make big changes. He told me that these are the most important areas the church must focus on now:

ACTION ITEMS

- Prioritizing ministry to children that focuses on instilling the Christian worldview.
- Teaching parents to more effectively raise their children to be "spiritual champions".
- Starting a Christian school, or at least doing more to support homeschooling parents.
- Making sure the discipleship model in every church means mature Christians sharing life one-on-one with those younger in the faith; holding them accountable to biblical principles.
- Teaching and preaching the Bible and not being afraid to tell members things they don't want to hear.

Ultimately, Dr. Barna says it comes down to making sure the church attracts rather than repels the lost and searching. "We did a big national study, we asked people across the country, 'What are the benefits that your community has received from having Christian churches located in your community?' Most Americans could not name a single benefit. We've got to change that. Can we be so focused on taking care of others that people say, 'Man, if we didn't have the church, we don't know what we'd do.'"

Utilizing the talent in the pews is a key part of making the church body more attractive. After all, what makes an organization stand out more than having a fully engaged membership? Unfortunately, too few senior pastors—or staff in general—are naturally open to seeking out talent and giving them the authority to use those God-given skills for the Body. An apt illustration is my experience several years ago.

There were some personnel issues impacting the church where my wife and I had recently joined. I was speaking with the senior pastor and asked, "Do you know that the former head of human resources for Union Carbide's worldwide operations is in a Sunday School class downstairs? He just might be able to help, don't you think?" The pastor was stunned but seemed interested, and I filled him in. He never reached out to that man; the personnel problems only got worse.

That's not an unusual story, according to Greg Ligon, a former pastor who for twenty-two years worked with Leadership Network; his last role was Chief Operating Officer for the organization whose mission is to strengthen church leaders. Greg and his wife Susan founded The Ligon Group, dedicated to helping leaders and organizations plan for the future and assisting in getting them there. He consistently says church staff must conduct what he calls "leadership discovery".

"If you look around, who are the people in your congregation that are leading groups of fifty somewhere? It may be their company, and maybe a Scout group and maybe the PTA or a sports league. They've already been equipped to train in leadership capacity. So how do we figure out how to unleash that capacity or harness that capacity for the church? That's one of the things I consider when

I think about high-capacity leaders. I think many churches do a poor job to be honest with you, engaging people that fall into this category.

"There's some intimidation that comes from the side of the senior pastor on occasion. The high-capacity leader, a corporate man or woman who's running a big company, is used to operating in a certain way. They become pretty impatient with the pace of church at times. I think the magic really happens whenever you begin to bridge that gap. The senior pastor begins to understand the value and is less threatened, and the high-capacity leader is able to operate within an adjusted pace."

That's why the first thing Greg asks when consulting a church is, "How do you develop leaders?" Unfortunately, the answers too many times illuminate the problem.

"I oftentimes we will get, 'Well, we do this thing, we do this, we do this, we do this.' And then one of the things I always ask is, 'Well, how's that being funded? Show me where that is in your budget.' It's very interesting, because it's very telling the churches that are really doing well understand the value of it—you're investing resources, and really helping to equip their people."

ACTION ITEM

Does your church have an up-to-date list of your members' vocations and interests, including a list of members leading groups of employees or volunteers? What's done with the information once you get it? Understanding what those talents in the pew are, and asking folks to be part of the mission, means giving up some control, finding out who can help, and turning them loose.

> **"My number one job as a pastor is not to minister."**
> —Pastor Dan Hall

Dan Hall has also been on both sides of the pulpit. He's pastored several large churches. Now, while leading a small start-up church in Madison, Mississippi, he also consults many others across the country. For years he's used Paul's letter to the leaders at the church of Ephesus as his guide: "And He Himself gave some to be apostles, some prophets, some evangelists, and some pastors and teachers, for the equipping of the saints for the work of ministry, for the edifying of the body of Christ."[20]

---

20 The Holy Bible, New Kings James Version (Nashville, TN, 1982) Ephesians 4:11-:12

"My number one job as a pastor is not to minister. My number one job is to *prepare you* to minister. That's my job. Now, as I tell some guys who try to sit in ivory towers and hide behind that, there's no way you can teach it if you're not doing it. But I don't do ministry because I'm a minister, I do ministry because I'm a believer. I train you to do ministry because I'm a minister."

Dan told me that those churches that haven't adjusted are going to suffer.

"That's where we get messed up. So we have everything backwards: the pew thinks we hire you to do ministry. I should be doing ministry because I'm a believer; you hire me to teach you to do ministry. You're freeing me up financially so that I can now mobilize the body of Christ. So I think the churches who were equipping their people to do ministry are going to be less impacted in the long term. Those who operated with a hierarchy, thinking every one of those pews existed to make my vision successful, are going to have to readjust significantly. Getting back to the biblical base, my job is to prepare you to impact the community."

Craig T. Owens is the pastor of Calvary Assembly of God in Cedar Springs, Michigan. He has also worked in a variety of leadership positions in the for-profit and non-profit worlds and recently wrote *Shepherd Leadership: The Metrics That Really Matter*. While discussing the book and key leadership traits, he quoted a former president from the 1950s.

"President Dwight Eisenhower said, 'If we ever think of

the United States as one leader and 158 million followers, it wouldn't be the United States.' I think the same thing in the church: if we think of it as being just one pastor—one minister—and then the rest of the congregation, it's not really a healthy church."

Craig sees himself as the shepherd, helping his members prepare to minister. That is a radical change from the top-down structure at so many churches. In these very challenging times, THE POST COVID CHURCH must be led by pastors willing to change and listen. Craig says it's not easy to hear constructive criticism.

"The bottom line is, I'm not going to change unless I want to change. If I'm not open to change, and if I don't have that kind of humility, or that posture, the words that other people speak aren't going to do anything to me."

Through his ministry, consulting work and research for his book, Craig knows a good church leader must be willing to listen to others.

"A senior pastor, or any senior leader, needs to be out among the people all the time, admitting mistakes, and letting people know, 'Hey, I was no good in this area. That's why I'm reading this book, or why I've gotten a mentor.' Those kinds of things will send the signal that says, 'I'm teachable. I'm open to learning, I'm willing to hear what other people have to say to me.' When a senior pastor gives up some of their authority, when they take their hands off some things, that also sends a signal of humble confidence. So I'd say if somebody's a leader—perhaps a lay leader in a church—if you hear those kind of statements coming from your pastor, your senior leader, then they probably are open to having further conversations about other things that need to be changed."

> **"I think for so long, Sunday morning has been our big production moment—for six days a week, we just focus on how to pull off Sunday. But that's backwards."**
>
> —Kelly Kannwischer | Future Church Co.

To reach outside the walls means making it a priority, reflected in both time and money spent. Effectively fulfilling the mission also means rethinking Sunday. Kelly Kannwischer is Co-founder and CEO of Future Church Co., which focuses on strengthening church leaders—staff and lay—and helping them lead congregations that more effectively fulfill the great commission: to make disciples. Kelly has effectively helped churches and non-profits tackle challenges by helping leaders lead effectively. For THE POST COVID CHURCH, it means that a bold vision requires much more than the Sunday service.

"Most of us think about doing worship, believing great worship will result in the mission of our church thriving. But we know that is not true. Real true growth starts with a culture of mission. When we focus on mission, you will get as an outflow, a robust expression of worship.... I think for so long, we've thought of Sunday morning as a big production moment, for six days a week, we just focus on how do we pull off Sunday? We've got to turn that upside down. We've got to think six days a week about how we're making disciples, out of which the overflow is we come together, and we worship meaningfully on Sunday."

Part of the problem is that so much energy and money have been spent not just on Sunday programs, but on buildings as well. Kelly says while there are certainly benefits for the Kingdom, too often the big picture is missed.

"A lot of the church growth movement in the second half of the twentieth-century did focus on helping to meet people's needs as the culture changed greatly. And you did see an incredible benefit of churches creating life centers. This was the big movement to have gyms and different ways for people to gather and to have fun together. And all of these things were good. C.S. Lewis talks about or warns against Christians having chronological snobbery, which is that we look backward and judge people. I don't want to do that in any way. But I think what we've learned is that, by themselves, these types of programs and emphasis on gathering and place aren't enough to equip people on the discipleship walk of today, given today's challenges, particularly since the digital revolution.

"So now that we are all connected to our phones and our screens, how now does the church need to innovate, to create meaningful relationships, connections and growth? And I think that's the opportunity in the future church."

For theologian and writer T.M. Moore, who I quoted

earlier in the book, this very Western, consumeristic tendency seeps into how we think about church.

"When people ask you, 'Where do you go to church?' we shouldn't answer by saying, 'I go to that church in that building over there.' We should have a different answer as to why I don't go *to* church: I *am* the church. I'm part of the church, all the church in this whole community. We tend to think in terms of buildings; we tend to think in terms of programs. We misconstrue the whole meaning of discipleship by making that sort of an optional choice for people; we offer programs. But then we say, 'If you want to come by, come, and if not, don't.' So eighty percent of people don't come.

"We're basically saying to them, 'You can define Christianity on your own terms, take as much or as little as you need of Christ and of this church. You'll be just fine, just as long as you come back next week. Oh, and don't go to the church down the road.'"

For T.M., the church has too quickly embraced what succeeds in the culture. The result is losing focus on what Christ calls the church to be.

"We're going to run programs, we're going to build buildings, we're going to hype our worship with all kinds of contemporary things. Whatever the scripture may have to say about these things will have to take second place behind what we choose to do. In the times in which we live, I think it's real evidence that we are captive to a culture, and we've lost sight of the plain teaching of Scripture on a lot of subjects."

ACTION ITEM

How much time, effort and staff time are dedicated to Sunday morning worship? How much time, money and effort are dedicated to making disciples? How is all that church space used? It won't take long to figure all this out. It will take much more time to focus on the real, important mission of the church. This is also a good exercise to get a firm grasp on what all the staff members are doing each day and week. If the work doesn't help the body of Christ make disciples, is it really needed?

> **"I think we need to expand the definition of what ministry is."**
>
> —Bishop Ronnie Crudup | Fellowship of International Churches

The pandemic has forced effective church leaders to reassess and pivot. Bishop Ronnie Crudup is Senior Pastor of New Horizon Church International in Jackson, Mississippi, and Administrative Bishop for the Fellowship of International Churches. He's spent his life in ministry and admits that THE POST COVID CHURCH means rethinking some basics.

"I think that we need to expand the definition of what ministry is. We talked about holistic ministry, but very often, I think we did certain things we were comfortable with. We've had to expand what we do and touch people in ways that we didn't touch them before. I think this is indicative of where the Lord wants us to go. And it's been gratifying to be involved."

For Bishop Crudup and his church, they had to more effectively embrace collaboration.

"Once again, back to that whole point of what change will mean to us. If we just go back into our corners, we don't really see the benefit of better collaboration, of bringing those walls down and crossing those barriers. I certainly have learned that lesson. I'm a lot more open to working with other people and I hope they will be with me as well."

Effective leadership means changing how an organization reacts during a crisis and adjusting people's duties to meet new needs. That's exactly what Lead Pastor Jonathan "J.P." Pokluda did at Harris Creek Baptist Church in Waco, Texas. With the doors shut, all the staff members had to add digital duties to their portfolio in order to reach the members. It also meant small groups, meeting away from the church, were critical if the community was to grow.

"Everybody had two jobs: they had their old job, and

then their new primary job. So their old job was their secondary job, and their new primary job was caring for life groups. We said, 'Hey, as these churches gather in homes and can't come in the building, we want to make sure that we're giving them exceptional care.' As our entire staff pivoted that way—everybody—we took all of the life groups and divided them amongst the number of staff people that we had. The staff's primary job was following up with those groups every week."

This change didn't just happen. In fact, just a few weeks before the COVID shutdown, J.P. told his church they had to be prepared.

"I just said, 'You know, we may not be able to gather here. There could be shifts in our government. There could be things that would make this illegal.' I then said, 'We won't miss a beat because we're going to continue to do church through the small groups.' That's how important life groups are. I was saying that to cast vision, and lo and behold, it happened shortly thereafter. We gathered the church and said, 'Hey, we won't be in this building for a while now. You guys really need to double down on your small groups.'"

ACTION ITEM

It will be all too easy for churches to simply slip back into old habits when the pandemic is in the rearview mirror. It's critical that THE POST COVID CHURCH focus on strengthening small groups and making sure they are at the center of the discipleship push. Does your church have a small group ministry? Is discipleship a cornerstone of this effort? Pastor Pokluda puts it so well in stressing that THE POST COVID CHURCH must get out of the consumer mindset of compartmentalizing our "church lives" to an hour or so on Sunday: "I'm just a simple guy, I teach the Bible, this is what the Bible says, this is what we'll do. I'm not calling people to come to church, I'm calling people to *be* the church, to *be* a part of this powerful movement that Jesus told us about two thousand years ago."

For T.M. Moore, this focus on small groups and the home, is, well, biblical.

"In the New Testament, you hear a lot of talk about churches in homes. That wasn't just because they didn't have buildings. That was simply the way the Lord wanted it to be done. The proof is the fact that the Christian movement grew and expanded for over two hundred years in that kind of a framework, before we really started seeing any church buildings in the Roman Empire. That, to me, indicates that this is a kind of a framework, a kind of a format, a template for doing church; dispersed in neighborhoods, in the homes of church leaders, that we should take into consideration."

Change is not easy—for anyone. There are also few leadership jobs tougher than senior pastor. Too often this book, as with any book that aims to help readers learn how to improve, can seem too negative, too full of bashing and not enough loving. Of course, none of us can get better unless we take that hard look in the mirror and open ourselves up to criticism from those we respect. On the other hand, it's more important than ever for senior pastors to have support and an outlet.

I earlier wrote about Greg Ligon's work with churches, helping them engage and empower the laity. When Greg and I spoke during our podcast, he said that one of the most fulfilling parts of his work is helping pastors find an outlet. Not just for their own good, but for the good of the congregation.

"What I continue to do in my work with Ligon Group is to create these cohorts, these opportunities for senior pastors—executive pastors—to be in the same room with one another. To learn from one another, to be able to have a safe place. They can talk about what's not working and what is working. That's really, really important.

"When I was at Leadership Network, we actually started what we called 'the next generation leader groups', and we did them for about a dozen years with close to four hundred senior pastors. This part of the work I was most proud about. If you look at the roster of those who participated, I can count on one hand the number that fell into some kind of moral situation or burned out. Of those few that had, most have been restored to ministry."

One of the countless benefits of talking to so many effective church leaders is understanding the key, foundational building blocks of effective churches. By effective, as we've seen, I don't mean attendance and budget numbers. It is effectiveness in living out Christ's great commission: making disciples. Dr. Bill Wilson, founder and CEO of the Center for Healthy Churches, comes from a long line of Baptist preachers and moved from leading churches to helping leaders from many different denominations. He quickly pointed out that there is one important facet of those that are successfully fulfilling the commission:

"The number one trait that I see in vibrant, transformed congregations of any stripe and flavor is *humility*. And a lot of that is born out of Jesus Christ as Lord. Meaning that we're renters; it's His operation. We're just stewards.

"That's one of the issues in our culture, too. People aren't humble enough to admit that maybe, whether we're talking about science or beliefs—maybe I'm wrong? Humility is not in a real, real big demand these days. So, we really are swimming upstream in culture because culture prizes pride, and pride demeans humility. That's been true from the beginning. Go back to Genesis; what got us in trouble was pride. It is our perpetual battle against the carnal self to replace that self-absorption and narcissism with absorption of God's agenda. Not 'What do I want?' But 'What does God need?' And that's a big transition."

Dr. Wilson agrees that the church cannot be content to try and "return to normal". First of all, that's impossible. It's also not what Christ demands the church to be. Dr. Wilson says all churches will fall into one of three modes: *resume, revise or relaunch.* Strong leadership will only pick the relaunch model—to embrace change. Yes, it's the most difficult and most humbling approach. It's also the only one that can help THE POST COVID CHURCH regain its influence for Christ in America.

CHAPTER FOUR:

Know What You Believe: Christian Worldview and Apologetics

Everybody has a worldview. Too few followers of Christ have a Christian worldview. That's a problem.

What is a worldview? Chuck Colson, the late Prison Fellowship founder who spent his last years teaching and preaching about the Christian worldview, called it "The sum total of our beliefs about the world, the 'big picture' that directs our daily decisions and actions."[21] It is the lens through which we look at the world and all the events that take place around us. That lens impacts how we interpret

21 Charles Colson and Nancy Pearcey, *How Now Shall We Live?*, (Carol Stream, Ill., Tyndale House Publishers, 1999), pp 14.

what we see. So, an atheist and a Christian will interpret a horrific crime or a sunset in vastly different ways.

> **"American Christianity is undergoing a 'post-Christian Reformation'—with the nation's major Christian groups rapidly replacing traditional theological beliefs with the culture's secular values."**
>
> —Dr. George Barna

Never in American history have those in power with non-Christian worldviews had such an impact on the nation. The naturalistic worldview, which rejects the possibility of anything supernatural and only believes what humans can determine by the five senses, successfully ran God out of the public schools. The postmodern worldview, which rejects the possibility of absolute truth and is built on the idea of relativism, created the idea of "my truth" to such an extent that even mathematics is now under fire for its rigidity. Sexual identity, once universally acknowledged as determined by chromosomes as either male or female, is now not based on science, but on how one "feels".

To see how much the secular culture has impacted the church, you only have to look at what Christians believe. Arizona Christian University's Dr. George Barna, who I quoted in Chapter three, has been researching Americans about faith for more than a generation. He told me he is devoting the rest of his career to making sure the American church understands how important it is that each member has a Christian worldview.

"Worldview is akin to a computer's operating system. If you have a computer without an operating system embedded in it, it can't do anything. A human being is the same way. You have to have something that's driving your decision making and that's what the worldview does. It helps you to understand experience, interpret and respond to all the different things in the world around you and helps you to figure out who you are. So if the church refuses to play the worldview development game, which up to this point it is refusing to do, the world takes over that job. That's why so few Christians have a biblical worldview."

Unfortunately, in America a shockingly small percentage of Christians have a Christian worldview. While that *should* sound axiomatic—like a professional football player saying he doesn't need to know or follow the football rules—it is in fact a reality. Here are some examples:

- Ligonier Ministries/Lifeway research in 2020 showed that:
  - 3 out of 10 *evangelical Christians* believe Christ was just a good teacher, not God.
  - Almost half of evangelicals believe humans are "good by nature."[22]

22 Ligonier Ministries, "The State of Theology," *https://thestateoftheology.com*, 2020

- A 2020 survey from the Cultural Research Center at Arizona Christian University showed that:
  * Among those attending evangelical churches, almost half believe *eternal salvation is earned* and that the Bible is not clear about whether *abortion is right or wrong.*
- More than one *out of three* believe:
  * *Lying is okay*
  * *Reject the traditional concept of marriage* and
  * Think it's *morally okay to abort a baby* if the birth will be a burden on the mother.
- More than half—52% of *evangelicals*—reject absolute moral truth.[23]

John Stonestreet, CEO of the Colson Center for Christian Worldview, says it's never been more important for Christians to both understand what a worldview is *and* to live out the Christian worldview. It's the only way THE POST COVID CHURCH can be stronger and more impactful.

"A Christian worldview is based on the truthfulness of Christianity, and what God has revealed in Scripture. What He's given to His church. What we know from the person of Jesus Christ in seeing all of reality, through that lens."

The Christian, grounded in the foundational precepts of the faith, should see a world created with purpose and inhabited with people all created in the image of God. From that critical understanding flows our values. As John

23 Arizona Christian University, "American Worldview Inventory 2020," *https:/ www.arizonachristian.edu/wp-content/uploads/2020/10/CRC_AWVI2020_Release11_Digital_04_20201006.pdf*, 2020

told me, what shapes the Christian worldview is the fact that our value as a person comes from God and is not earned, nor does it come from what we do.

"These are very different visions of the world; whether morality is baked into the universe, like gravity, or whether morality changes from person to person or culture to culture. Also, whether history is headed towards some sort of economic utopia, as the Marxist would say, or whether it's headed to some sort of kind of disembodied return to the universal spirit, as Hindus would say. Or whether there is a restoration, a process by which the things that are wrong are going to be made right. These are very different visions for life in the world."

It's especially important that teaching about worldviews and emphasizing Christian worldview education be a priority for youth ministry. Once they leave the safe, secure cocoon of their local church, research shows that most teens will drift away from the faith. That's why Dr. Corey Miller is leading Ratio Christi, which is Latin for the "Reason of Christ". The group's motto, "Thoughtful Christianity—Transforming Lives on Campus Today, Changing Culture Tomorrow", is focused on transforming colleges and university students and faculty because, Dr. Miller told me, the church has failed.

"The evangelical church has been relatively good at exhibiting the hand of Christ and the heart of Christ. But in some cases, it can be argued that we have excommunicated the head of Christ. What we want is a fully-integrated Christian."

The big problem: youth ministry not preparing students.

"They don't know what they believe in, why they believe it. They can't defend what they believe. They leave their safe, secure nest of what they've taken for granted at their home church, with a youth pastor focusing more on skinny jeans and fog machines than on substance. They get to this place called the university and we quickly find that the church has not done its job."

> **"If churches are not including apologetics, across the board at virtually all age ranges now in our secularizing culture, they are not doing their jobs."**
>
> —Dr. Corey Miller | Ratio Christi

"We need to be equipping our people for works of ministry, and not only equipping them for survival. We don't want them to simply survive in these hostile environments, but to thrive. The non-believing world wants reasoned answers. Now, that doesn't mean we have to throw away the hands of Christ and the heart of Christ. It simply means we need to readmit into fellowship the head of Christ, and love God with our mind as Jesus commanded. So not only is apologetics back in demand, it's still a command, as we see in First Peter 3:15."

Apologetics is the art of defending the Christian faith. For Greg Koukl, it's a passion. He is a nationally known apologist who founded Stand to Reason in order to help Christians think more clearly about their faith. He effectively uses debates, podcasts, radio shows and books to not just explain why Christianity makes sense, but also how to equip followers of Christ to better explain and defend the faith. He knows a big problem is when any Christian, but especially the young, brings tough questions to the church. Too often, Greg told me, pastors, staff and teachers refuse to dig deeply and are unprepared to answer those disturbing questions.

"The evangelical church has just been too satisfied with, 'I've been saved and that's the Good News', and doesn't want to think about what those tough issues are."

The youth are bombarded by competing worldviews and understandably have questions. It's normal to hear those challenges to the faith and to have doubts. Greg says far too often, these proper questions are met with resistance or worse: accusations that those with questions don't have enough faith or are troublemakers.

"These kids are now ripe for picking from either progressive Christianity or the culture, which is really mounting an aggressive challenge to virtually everything that we believe as foundational to Christianity."

The pressure to reject the basic tenets of the Christian faith continue to mount. That is why THE POST COVID CHURCH must better prepare all Believers. It's why Greg says pastors and teachers must know what they believe and be able to defend it. Never has the church in America faced such challenges.

"I think the pastors just don't know any better, and they're nervous. So they just tell people to be quiet. That's a huge problem. We want pastors to be able to say, 'Look, it's okay if you have questions and doubts.' It doesn't have to be debilitating. Everybody has dealt with it. That's normal. Even atheists have doubts."

> **"When people are attacking our very core beliefs, or when one way of viewing and understanding the world is staring down the Christian way of viewing and understanding the world, we have to go deeper."**
>
> —Dr. Matt Ayars | Wesley Biblical Seminary

Understanding that the Bible isn't a nice book with encouraging stories, but rather Holy Scripture and the Word of God, leads to not just a stronger Christian faith. It also feeds a more robust Christian worldview. That's never been more important than now, says Dr. Matt Ayars, President of Wesley Biblical Seminary in Jackson, Mississippi. He is encouraged that seminaries such as WBS are expanding beyond preparing men and women for full-time ministry. Providing online and in-person educational opportunities for lay church members is better preparing all Christians to understand and answer our culture's challenge to basic, foundational Christian beliefs.

"We're in the height of this culture war, one worldview against another worldview. These questions that feed into this culture war and this worldview issue, they get at the very core tenets of what we believe. Unfortunately, too many times the standard sermons are on, for example, five ways to fix a marriage, or healthy finances, or how to manage stress. Now, addressing those topics is fine. But when people are attacking our very core beliefs, or when one way of viewing and understanding the world is staring down the Christian way of viewing and understanding the world, we have to go deeper to understand what it is that through the centuries Christians have believed and why."

That means making sure THE POST COVID CHURCH does not back away from biblical teaching in the pulpit, in small groups and in Sunday school. Dr. Ayars says that focus will provide critical instruction on how to answer those challenges.

"There's more of a demand now than ever, in the midst of a culture war, to be able to have the answers to these questions. The first thing we do is turn back to the Scriptures to ask, 'What does Jesus tell us? What is our tradition? Tell us through the scriptures about these sorts of things, these questions that are at the heart of helping us navigate these issues.' The Apostle Paul says to consider it a blessing when you face adversity, when you face difficulty. The challenges that force us to go deeper is one reason why it is a blessing. Seminaries are there to help us go deeper because you have people in the church who have already explored these questions through their training."

Helping the lay members to access and understand more about the Bible and how it relates means THE POST COVID CHURCH will produce more Christians with a strong Christian worldview.

ACTION STEPS

Does your church ever teach about worldviews, specifically how the Christian worldview compares to others? If this is not part of the teaching and preaching for all age groups, your church will be ill-equipped to answer the secular culture's influence. There are many Christian organizations, such as the Colson Center for Christian Worldview, that provide educational material to help your church leaders incorporate worldview teaching. Groups such as Greg Koukl's Stand to Reason have lots of material to help build an apologetics curriculum at your church. It does no good to complain about the direction of our nation's morals if the church isn't prepared to answer the challenge. For THE POST COVID CHURCH to regain its influence, worldview education has to be a priority.

CHAPTER FIVE

Image Problem: Time To Admit It and Take (often unpleasant) Stands

The first chapter of this book outlines the radical shift the American culture has taken when it comes to the waning influence of orthodox Christian beliefs in the public square. The fact is, the term "evangelical Christian" has never been so tied to politics, and that will impact how THE POST COVID CHURCH fulfills its mission of making disciples and being the hands and feet of Christ outside the church walls.

Before looking more closely at the trends, it's important to agree on definitions. In 2015, the National Association of Evangelicals and Lifeway Research developed and published this definition of evangelical belief. Someone is labeled as "evangelical by belief" if they strongly agree that:

- The Bible is the highest authority for what I believe.
- It is very important for me personally to encourage non-Christians to trust Jesus Christ as their Savior.
- Jesus Christ's death on the cross is the only sacrifice that could remove the penalty of my sin.
- Only those who trust in Jesus Christ alone as their Savior receive God's free gift of eternal salvation.[24]

About twenty percent—one in five—of American adults have consistently been identified as evangelicals by this definition. Not surprisingly, if you look at folks who "self-identify" as evangelical, there are more of them, although the number of self-identified evangelicals is dropping.

According to Gallup, 34% of Americans in 2020 identified themselves as "evangelical", a drop of ten percentage points in just six years and the fewest self-described evangelicals in the almost twenty-year history of the survey. The Public Religion Research Institute showed the number of white evangelicals also falling to a record low of fewer than 15%, dropping almost in half since 2006.[25] Now, social scientists have questions about the polling methods; that's

24 Aaron Earls, "Who Are 'Evangelicals' and Why Knowing That Matters for Your Church", Lifeway Research, *https://lifewayresearch.com/2021/07/26/who-are-evangelicals-and-why-knowing-that-matters-for-your-church/*, 06.26.2021

25 PRRI Staff, "The 2020 Census of American Religion", Public Religion Research Institute, *https://www.prri.org/research/2020-census-of-american-religion/, 07.08.2021*

always the case when you're trying to put a firm figure on a group whose identity is defined in some broad ways. The important point is, the consensus of surveys during the last several decades undeniably shows that Christianity is waning in America.

What has not dropped is the strikingly political affiliation of evangelicals. In the 2020 election, as noted in Chapter one, four out of five white evangelicals voted for President Trump.[26] The very strong affiliation between evangelicals, however they are defined, and the GOP has created a strong voting block and impacted how the evangelical church is viewed and operates. Just as the African American voters in America have been overwhelmingly aligned with the Democratic party—by about the same 80% margin[27]—the power of any one group within a political party means more suspicion and mistrust of those outside that party.

For a secular group, this overwhelming connection to one political party can been seen as simply the cost of doing business.

For Christianity, it marks an obstacle to evangelism. Christ showed the church what it means to speak "truth to power": you were either a follower or not. While always communicating with grace and love, Christ pulled no punches, no matter how powerful the target. Christ's church is also expected to speak the truth and power of

26 Elana Schor and David Crary, "AP VoteCast: Trump wins White Evangelicals, Catholics Split", AP Votecast, *https://apnews.com/article/votecast-trump-wins-white-evangelicals-d0cb249ea7eae29187a21a702dc84706,* 11.06.2020

27 Ismail K. White and Chryl N. Laird, "Why Are Blacks Democrats", Princeton, *https://press.princeton.edu/ideas/why-are-blacks-democrats,* 02.25.2020

the Word—and call what is unrighteous unrighteous—no matter the political affiliation of the subject.

This is no way means abandoning Christian principals. It also does not mean that Christians are not to be involved in the political process. It *does* mean that the evangelical church must realize that there is a major barrier that needs to be crossed. It means building bridges to serve, taking time to listen and following Christ's example by engaging with those who don't believe as you do. One good example comes from the heart of secularism: Los Angeles.

> **"Pro-choice friends ask, 'What do you do for women who are homeless?' We're here to help."**
>
> —Ali Kellogg | Harvest Home

Harvest Home is a non-denominational, faith-based non-profit that houses homeless pregnant women and their babies in Los Angeles.

Harvest Home gets all its money from donors. Happily, during the pandemic, more people have stepped up to help because they see the local need. "During COVID there have been a lot of inquiries about homelessness and how to help," says Harvest Home Outreach & Events Manager Ali Kellogg. "Homelessness is such a crisis in L.A. and it's even worse now. A lot of people have a heart for that. People wanted to make tangible donations. Yes, we still get financial gifts, but more wanted to donate items for the moms and their babies. While those who are giving are also seeing financial uncertainty, it is important for them to know exactly how their money is being used."

One example: for the first pandemic Thanksgiving, Harvest Home sent an email asking for donations to buy turkeys for the women, and $3,000 was raised in an hour. In this heart of pro-choice land, Ali says support for the ministry providing life is striking. "Moms understand the need for housing for pregnant women. Who can argue with helping homeless women who are pregnant? Pro-choice friends ask, 'What do you do for women who are pregnant and in situations where they can't support a baby?' Harvest Home is one answer of how we're here to help."

ACTION STEP

Christ was constantly pushing Believers out of their comfort zone. To follow Him meant not just taking up the cross daily, but also living a life diametrically opposed to that of the culture. Far too often the American church has been satisfied to remain in its comfort zone. Does your church reach outside the walls to not just help the needy, but engage? What a perfect time to, for example, get together with a church of another race to honestly talk about differences and make disciples together. Leaders need to ask, "What is it we can do that will make those without Christ stand up, notice and engage?"

It's already clear that for a myriad of reasons the American church is smaller since the pandemic hit. As noted earlier in the book, research from The Barna Group found that one out of three church members quit attending in person or on-line once the shutdown hit in the spring of 2020.[28] The consensus of all the experts I interviewed is that THE POST COVID CHURCH will be smaller. The silver lining? In the face of persecution, hostility and disinterest, the church has the opportunity to be stronger.

Rev. Dr. Randy Russ is a lifelong evangelical Methodist and commissioned deacon with the United Methodist Church, and holds a Ph.D. in marketing. His career has spanned business (he was President and CEO of Community Coffee), academia (business professor at Belhaven and Jackson State Universities) and the ministry (executive pastor at Christ United Methodist Church, one of the largest congregations in Mississippi). Dr. Russ now lives in Louisiana and sees good coming out of small.

"It's been said for many years that recessions cut the wheat from the chaff. During a recession, weak businesses tend to struggle even more and often fail. I think this is a recession that's been induced due to public policy. So churches who were struggling before are going to have a very difficult time coming out of this. Many denominations were already in membership declines, with giving and average church attendance in decline for decades. I think churches that don't take this as an opportunity to

---

28 *Barna: State of the Church*, "One in Three Practicing Christians Has Stopped Attending Church During COVID-19", *https://www.barna.com/research/new-sunday-morning-part-2/*, 7.08.2020

really reflect on what they need to change probably will not make it in the long term."

For Dr. Russ, the good news will be evident in the churches that innovate.

"People will be searching for answers that Christians have—the good news of Jesus Christ. Sharing the good news with others that God has for us. He is with us even through these challenging times. I think churches that were inwardly focused, staff-driven, institutional model churches will not be able to minister to those who are seeking."

Dr. Russ agrees that THE POST COVID CHURCH must take a hard look at itself and change.

"I think churches would be wise to shift from a staff-driven focus to engaging, equipping and empowering the laity—the priesthood of the believers—to engage in the ministry. That's because the institutional church model, over the last fifty years in mainline denominations, has been a failure. In every statistic you could look at."

> **"Where the real problems start coming in, is when we get fat, stupid and lazy."**
>
> —Fr. Daniel Dower

The pandemic has made even the most top-down organizations rethink how things are done. Fr. Daniel Dower is not just a pastor and President of St. Mary's Catholic

Church and School in Longview, Texas, he's also a doctoral student whose research focuses on what THE POST COVID CHURCH must look like if it is to fulfill its mission of making disciples. "Don't be afraid of the fact that you may have to jettison that idea and move on to something else. It's opening up a whole new way of doing ministry," Fr. Dower told me.

What a refreshing outlook! Father Dower says we've all been shaken and likens our challenges to a nursery rhyme.

"One of my doctoral professors says, 'Where the real problems start coming in, is when we get fat, stupid and lazy.' That when things are easy, when everything's going fine, we think we don't need God—until a little virus shows up. Then we realize, 'Oh, wait a minute. Well, I didn't mean that.'

"I was getting ready for my paper and I thought, 'Ah, Humpty Dumpty sat on a wall. Humpty Dumpty had a great fall. All the king's horses, all the king's men, couldn't put Humpty together again.' I saw that little Mother Jones nursery rhyme as being an encapsulation of where we are.

"Who's Humpty Dumpty? Humpty Dumpty was our comfortable way of living. Humpty Dumpty was that nice little neat package, that nice smooth little egg. Yes, we had to be careful with it. Yes, you needed to let in just enough air and just enough light to stay alive. But we put it up on a wall, out of reach of everyone else, because we're happy with the way things are. Don't break it, leave it alone. And then what happened? It fell."

This lack of control, facing what seems like a never-ending

stream of uncertainty, is certainly not what Americans are used to.

"We couldn't do anything about it, and that egg broke into a million pieces. Our leadership, going into the future, has to be far more inclusive and far less concerned about getting everything perfect. So instead of being so vertical, we need to start being far more horizontal, and take the things down off the shelf, off the wall, and put them down on the street level. Don't be afraid of the fact that you may have to jettison that idea and move on to something else. It's opening up a whole different way of doing ministry."

> **"Thanks, Jesus, that's great. But you know what? We have some good ideas too."**
>
> —T.M. Moore | The Fellowship of Ailbe

Of course, changing direction takes strong leadership, as we looked at in Chapter three. It also means all Believers must be willing to put aside all their assumptions and ideas that don't conform to the Bible. T.M. Moore, in an earlier chapter, spoke about how leadership must break out of the Western mindset. He also says we all must relinquish control.

"Jesus says, 'I will build my church. And here's what worship looks like. And here's what disciple making looks like. And here's what mission looks like.' And we say, 'Thanks,

Jesus, that's great. But you know what? We have some good ideas too.' And our good ideas are, frankly, causing us to fall way behind. Even to the point where the underbelly of this culture that is now showing itself in such ugly fashion during this time, the responsibility and the blame for that in many ways is laid at the feet of the church. We have failed to be the salt and light and leaven that we've been called to be, because we're so bound up in the culture of our time that we can't be the church that Christ has made us to be. I'm a little bit passionate about this."

For centuries the Christian church on "mission" has been the hands and feet of Christ to those who were in desperate need of the Gospel and lifesaving help. For example, hospitals were created because Christians saw a tremendous need and were able to serve all those made in "the image of God."

Well, mission is now changing.

The pandemic slammed the door on short-term mission trips outside America. Duane Brown is Director of Church Partnership for OMS International, which for decades has sent men and women around the world to serve. Just as churches pivoted to digital communication, so did OMC in order to stay connected. It also means sharing with the church unique ways to mission: instead of taking Americans to Asia, for example, Duane says the church can serve Asians in America.

"How can we take teams from one state to another, to minister to people from Asia living in the United States? In other words, there are all kinds of opportunities for the church, domestically, in our own backyards. There are people from other countries that we can minister to, that we can love on with the love of Jesus Christ."

THE POST COVID CHURCH must, of course, remain focused on making disciples around the world. Duane says the pandemic has opened up new opportunities to do much more than make short-term trips. It has reinforced the importance of raising up leaders for Christ overseas.

"That is the heart of sound missiology now, and that's been the heart of missiology going way back to the early 1900s. When our founders, Charles and Lettie Cowman, launched their ministry into Asia, the passion was not to do ministry for the Japanese. It was to raise up the sons and daughters of Japan to fulfill the great commission among their people. That is the heart of good missiology in today's culture; that we are raising up indigenous people to lead and grow a movement. We come alongside them and pray for them, encourage them and equip them to do the job of launching a movement of Christianity among their own people."

> **"Churches that are outward-focused make a difference. Churches that are inward-focused will eventually die."**
>
> — Rev. Dr. Warren Lathem | Venezuela Now

We in America can also learn from the church overseas. Rev. Dr. Warren Lathem spent almost half a century as a

United Methodist pastor and district superintendent. He also started Venezuela Now in 1996 and is the group's President. The organization supports various ministries and a seminary in that impoverished South American country. Shortly after the shutdown in America, Dr. Lathem was disappointed to see so many churches turn in and wait for "normal" to return. He was excited, however, to see the church in Venezuela reach out during the shutdown. How? By bringing church into the home.

"Uncle Joe doesn't go to church, but church is in his house now, and he's hearing the Gospel for the first time. Children are hearing the Gospel for the first time. There were so many conversions that the bishop said they will be planting new churches when this pandemic is over.

"Another example is the pastor going up on the rooftops of Venezuela, preaching in the evenings, to a number of people who have not heard the Gospel. One American pastor heard that and said, 'I'm ashamed, because some of my neighbors said to me, 'Why haven't we already been doing this?' We've got to be more conscious about getting into our own neighborhoods."

Dr. Lathem says THE POST COVID CHURCH must be more intentional when it comes to mission and disciple making.

"There has to be a theological foundation that is clearly laid out in the congregation by the pastor as to the mission of the church. Churches are often everything to everybody and nothing to nobody. It takes a concerted effort: education, training, preaching and leading to get a church to understand that our mission is to make disciples. It is the core of what we do. It's out *there*, not in here. It's not about us, it's about *them*. So how do we turn the focus from inward-focused to outward-focused? The biggest difference I see in churches today is the choices they make, either actively or passively. The choice is that outward-focused churches make a difference. Churches that are inward-focused will eventually die."

ACTION STEP

During the pandemic, ironically, mission was all too often put on the back burner or ignored completely despite the greater need! Duane Brown from OMS says now is the time for THE POST COVID CHURCH to get members thinking about mission.

"I think we need to ask ourselves as church leaders, 'How can we inspire and communicate mission to our people?' I think one of the greatest roadblocks to people not engaging in the work of the church, its mission, is the fact that they're not inspired. They don't know what's happening. There's no clear communication strategy, one that casts vision and inspires people to greater involvement. How much time do you set aside in your church calendar on a weekly basis to communicate the mission of your church, to inspire people to become personally engaged in that mission and connected to it? That's the question I would leave: how can we better inspire and communicate mission to our people?"

The rapid secularization and hostility towards Christianity in America is not likely to subside. In fact, it is rapidly growing in pace and influence. Christ reminds us, "Fear not." THE POST COVID CHURCH must acknowledge the image problem of its own creation and, more importantly, be focused on how to serve in such a way that even the most strident among the "haters" can't help but sit up, notice and acknowledge that those Christians *aren't afraid* to engage and make a difference.

CHAPTER SIX

Not Just Surviving but THRIVING!

Back in 1961 the Green Bay Packers opened training camp months after blowing a late lead and losing the NFL Championship game to the Philadelphia Eagles. The Packers' head coach, the legendary Vince Lombardi, knew he had players talented enough to win it all, but he'd seen them fall short. So, at the first practice of the new season, Coach Lombardi looked at this group of grown men who'd played football just about all their lives, raised his hands and, pointing to what he was holding, said, "Gentlemen, this is a football."

The Green Bay Packers were getting back to basics. It's an apt illustration for THE POST COVID CHURCH. With membership declining, impact waning and antagonism against the church growing, this is the time to make sure the foundation of the church is firm. It is especially important as the young leave the church in unprecedented numbers with no reason to believe that they will return.

The last thing Christ instructed his disciples to do was *make disciples*. Out of this effort will come a stronger church, with members impacting the needy, hurting and lost. First, as Christ said, we must be His disciples. Kelly Kannwischer's Future Church Co. helps churches fulfill their mission by making sure everything they do points to discipleship. She explains that all churches have a "lower room" with the four Ps:

Place
Personality
Programs
People

"These are things that are good, but we want to help people reach what we call the upper room, which is the disciple-making capacity of the church.... So that's the mission of the church, that's the reason the church exists: to fulfill the Great Commission. And every church names their local mission differently, but that's the purpose. And what we do is try to help churches build the staircase. How are you intentionally moving people from that lower room to the upper room, from the experience of Church to the disciple walk with Jesus? And that's our mission."

The problem, of course, is that it's more fun and lot easier to do all the stuff in the lower room. T.M. Moore says far too often, churches don't even bother making that connection to discipleship.

"It's every person having someone over them, to nurture them in the faith of our Lord Jesus Christ. It's a personal relational oversight of people, caring for them, building them up in the Lord, and then the most holy faith. But that's not what we do. First of all, we define discipleship; we don't define *what a disciple is* very well. We then make discipleship optional by offering programs that people can sign up for if they want to. We leave it to them to make themselves disciples, rather than to put them under the caring love of shepherds who are working daily to make them disciples."

The church in America isn't just shrinking, it's getting older—much older. Historically young adults have drifted away from the church, only to return when the children arrived. That is not the case now, and it will not change unless THE POST COVID CHURCH gets more intentional.

For more than a decade Probe Ministries has studied the younger generation. A 2020 survey[29] showed that those aged 18-29 who are not affiliated with a church almost tripled (from 13% to 35% of the population). Of greater concern, when comparing those in their twenties back in 2010 to those in their thirties a decade later, are these numbers:

- Those classified as "Born Again" Christians dropped from 27% to 22%.

---

29 Steve Cable, "Religious Views and Practices: 2020", Probe for Answers, *https://probe.org/introducing-probes-new-survey-religious-views-and-practices-2020/*, 06.30.2021

- Reading their Bible at least once a week dropped from 14% to 10%.
- Those who believe in four key biblical beliefs[30] plummeted from 12% to 5%.

Probe ministry's very reasonable conclusion: with unaffiliated numbers rising and born-again Christians with an active faith declining, young adults are not returning to the faith as they move into their thirties.

Many attribute the loss of young evangelicals to their more accepting views regarding sexuality, specifically gay marriage. In fact, while more Americans than ever support gay marriage, the young have always been more supportive than the old.[31] Yes, sudden freedom when leaving home plays a part. The big reason the young people are leaving the church and not returning, however, is because the ministry programs aren't designed to build that Christian worldview. In Chapter four, Ratio Christi's Dr. Corey Miller explained that his group's vision, "Thoughtful Christianity—Transforming Lives on Campus Today, Changing Culture Tomorrow", is much harder because of the thin biblical gruel fed to so many teens. This has led to

---

30 1. Which of the following descriptions comes closest to what you personally believe to be true about God: God is the all-powerful, all knowing, perfect creator of the universe who rules the world today. 2. The Bible is totally accurate in all of its teachings: Strongly Agree 3. If a person is generally good enough or does enough good things for others during their life, they will earn a place in heaven: Disagree Strongly 4. When He lived on earth, Jesus Christ committed sins like other people: Disagree Strongly

31 Justin McCarthy, "Record High 70% in U.S. Support Same-Sex Marriage", Gallup, *https://news.gallup.com/poll/350486/record-high-support-same-sex-marriage.aspx*, 06.08.2021

a rejection of biblical beliefs and the embrace of the culture's focus on "self".

ACTION STEPS

The effort to entice youth through "hip" ministers, rock-style music and ignoring difficult biblical passages clearly isn't working. Not just teaching young members about faith, but also why Christians believe in fundamental beliefs must be incorporated early in every church. The culture is embracing "feelings" as the driving force behind decision making. That's an un-Christian approach that must be attacked head on. As the research about youth—and church members in general—has shown in this book, very few Christians have a Christian worldview. Without it, there is no hope of retaining even the basic tenets of the faith in the face of the secular worldview. It also means openly, transparently wrestling with these tough issues.

CONCLUSION

Despite the challenges facing THE POST COVID CHURCH, the men and women I spoke with are optimistic. It's not that they deny there will be troubles. Rather, they firmly believe the Lord is in control, and that this is a time for the church to stand out. The numbers clearly show that the church is shrinking. The church in America will also face an increasingly hostile government.

> **"What you're going to see is the destruction of cultural Christianity, and out of that will remain vibrant, historic, orthodox Christianity."**
>
> —S. Michael Craven | Colson Center for Christian Worldview

S. Michael Craven, Director of the Colson Fellows Program at the Colson Center for Christian Worldview, is an executive, a worldview expert, cultural apologist, and author. His eyes are wide open about the challenges, and he says Christians must be prepared for hostility. He told me that THE POST COVID CHURCH cannot lose sight of the big picture.

"I don't think it's going to be the kind of persecution that we read about frequently around the world or throughout history. I think it will be for most Americans at a point of particular pain and pressure, because it'll be largely economic. We're already seeing that."

An example Michael points out is Twitter in January 2021 suspending the account of *The Dispatch*, a conservative online magazine, for simply describing one of President Biden's nominees: "On Tuesday, President-elect Joe Biden announced that he had chosen Dr. Rachel Levine to serve as Assistant Secretary for Health at the Department of HHS. Dr. Levine is a transgender woman; that is, a man who believes he is a woman".

The magazine's definition of transgender got it the boot. As the "cancel culture" spreads, it does not make Michael pessimistic. In fact, it encourages him.

"In this nation, I'm more encouraged than I've ever been. I think that is only possible due to the pressure imposed by the persecution, by the marginalization, by the pulling back of the veil and the pretense and saying, 'You know what, we're not even going to pretend to be Christian anymore. We don't like you. We don't like what you stand for. We stand in direct opposition to all your claims as Christians.' Well, the line of demarcation is becoming clearer and clearer and clearer. What you're going to see is the destruction of cultural Christianity, and out of that will remain vibrant, historic, orthodox Christianity."

Will this post-cultural Christianity be ushered in through another revival? There are many who pray that is the case. T.M. Moore says that unfortunately, too many think of revival as an *event*. As history shows, the biggest American revivals, the Great Awakening and the Second Great Awakening, did in fact rock the culture and usher in a more vibrant church. It also began with Believers repenting.

"I think many people, when they think of the term *revival*, people who've grown up in the church think of a week of meetings with a special guest speaker. There's a lot of organization. There's food that has to be gathered, the announcements have to get out and we're going to have a week of meetings. Then when that's over, nothing much happens as a result."

T.M. says it is critical that the church stop thinking of a revival as something *we* do.

"The teaching of Scripture is quite the contrary, that revival is something that God does. He begins it in the hearts of each one of His people, and in their churches. They actually experience a greater quickening in the life of faith, have a larger view and a richer experience of their salvation. That then begins to flow out from them to the larger world. This is something that God does. He does it in His timing. He does it in His way. And when He does it, there's no mistaking that something unique is going on here."

Every revival also begins with repentance. Evangelist Rodney "Gipsy" Smith was once asked how to start a revival. He said, "Go back to your home and draw a circle around you on the floor. Then get down on your knees in the middle of the circle and ask God to convert everybody inside that circle."[32]

"It has to begin in us, and God is not going to revive us if we're holding onto sin," T.M. told me. "If we insist on continuing in those ways which are inimical to following Him, then there's not going to be any revival. Psalm 66:18 says if we harbor sin in our lives, God won't even hear our prayers, much less answer them. So there has to be confession of sin, there has to be waiting on the Lord to convict us and to admit our sins, and then it's necessary to make restoration within the parameters of those sins. If I've sinned against you, I need to come to you; we need to be healed peaceably together as a result of that confession, leading to the kind of penance or a practice of a different way of life. That allows that healing to take place. If we're just looking for that as some sort of a patch to the kind of compromised Christianity we've been living all of our lives, that's not going to happen."

It will take not just right thinking, but right action for THE POST COVID CHURCH to thrive and not simply survive. Having a Christian worldview and doing nothing with it defeats God's purpose for the church! It also means not being overwhelmed by all that is happening in Washington, D.C.

John Stonestreet, CEO of the Colson Center for Christian

32 Pastor Dewey Moede, For God's Glory Alone Ministry, "You Want A Revival?", *https://www.fggam.org/2014/03/the-quote-of-the-day-you-want-a-revival/*, 3.28.2014

Worldview, told me about one big problem: the last few decades have seen so much of our life being nationalized. Big Box stores, franchise restaurants and Hollywood culture have come to dominate. It's left what he calls "the middle" hollowed out. THE POST COVID CHURCH must aggressively act.

"If you find yourself in the middle, then steward the middle. Bring restoration and redemption to the middle. I think we've seen that on a number of levels the inability, for example, of churches to deal with local communities in the midst of this crisis. It has ended up in an unbelievable spike in suicides and mental illness. In other words, these are the side effects of COVID that have nothing to do with COVID whatsoever. They have to do with the isolation."

As mentioned in Chapter two, there is so much the church can do to help those isolated. For example, a simple phone tree where fellow church members reach out to speak with those who are homebound. John says it's often the simple things that Believers can do that will fill the empty middle.

"That's where the church can reach out to the hurting. That's where the church can provide help. It has something to do with the church remembering the localized work that it's been called to do. I think that's a feature of American culture that has misled us. We need to go back to it. Once we start there, once we start looking around and saying, 'Well, what good can I do?', then we'll stop asking the question, 'What's all the good that we *can't* do?' It's not like, 'Well, I can't change this, and I can't change that.'

There's so much we can change."

That means rethinking and acting. It won't be easy and won't feel good. Bishop Crudup from The Fellowship of International Churches is optimistic that THE POST COVID CHURCH will be stronger *because* of the discomfort.

"The reality is we needed to change, all of us needed to change. I don't care how much success you typically thought you have, we all needed to change. This thing is stretching us, pushing us, forcing us into circumstances that we may not have been as comfortable with as those at the very beginning. But I think we'll come out of this so much better."

May that be the impact the world sees from THE POST COVID CHURCH.

INDEX

Arizona Christian University 51, 70, 72
Ayars, Matt 76-77

Barna, George 51-53, 70-71
Barna Research 24, 84
Biden, Joe 100
Brown, Duane 88-89, 91
Bush, George W. 23

Carter, Jimmy 22-23
Chapman, Ken 47
Colson, Chuck 48, 69
Cowman, Charles and Lettie 89
Craven, S. Michael 99-100
Crudup, Ronnie 62-63, 104

Dower, Daniel 85-87

Eisenhower, Dwight D. 57

Falwell, Jerry 23
Ferguson, Niall 27
Fleming, Tarama 37
Friedrich, Elaine 35-36
Friedeman, Matt 45-47

Gallup Poll 19-20, 80

Hahn, Robert 41-43
Hall, Dan 56-57
Hattersley, Roy 28
Henderson, Chip 33

Kannwischer, Kelly 59, 94
Kellogg, Ali 82-83
Koukl, Gary 74-76

Lathem, Warren 89-91
Levine, Rachel 100
Lifeway Research 71, 79-80
Ligon, Greg 54-55, 66
Ligon, Susan 54
Logonier Ministries 71
Lombardi, Vince 93
Luther, Martin 46

McCray, Percy 38
Miller, Corey 73-74, 96
Moore, T.M. 31, 49, 60-61, 65, 87-88, 94-95, 101-102
Murray, Douglas 27

National Association of Evangelicals 79-80

Obama, Barack 23
Owens, Craig T. 57-59

Pew Research 24
Phillips, Jack 24
Pierre, Lucner 33
Pokluda, Jonathan 63-65
Public Religion Research Institute 80
Probe Ministry 95

Rabon, Rusty 43
Reagan, Ronald 22
Robertson, John 50
Russ, Randy 84-85

Sayers, Mark 22
Schaeffer, Francis 21-22
Smith, Rodney "Gipsy" 101
Southern Baptist 24
Stonestreet, John 72-73, 102-103
Stradinger, Joe 32

The Dispatch 100
Trump, Donald 23, 80
Twitter 100

Van Maren, Jonathon 27

Wadner, David 37, 39
Walker, Phil 44-45
Wilson, Bill 18, 67-68
Wright, N.T. 27

Made in the USA
Columbia, SC
20 October 2021

47195611R00061